LIFE

Descending / Ascending

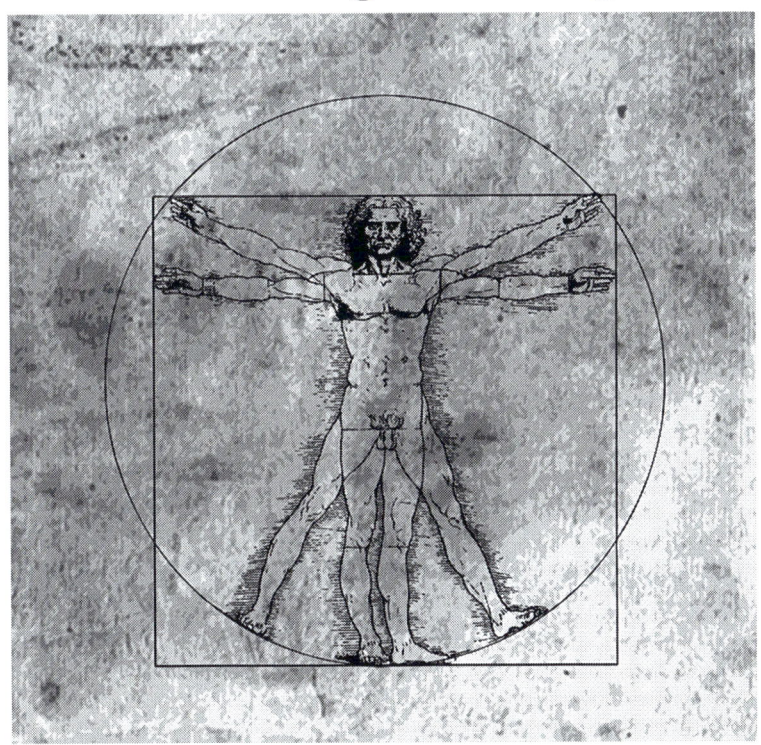

Alice Shapiro

TotalRecall Publications

United States of America

Canada, and United Kingdom.

Copyright© 2010 by: Alice Shapiro

All rights reserved. Except as permitted under the United States Copyright Act of 1976, No part of this publication may be reproduced, stored in a retrieval system, or transmitted in any form or by any means electronic or mechanical or by photocopying, recording, or otherwise without the prior permission of the publisher.

ISBN: 978-1-59095-778-3

UPC 6-43977-27784-8

Exclusive Worldwide publication and distribution by
TotalRecall Publications, Inc
1103 Middlecreek Friendswood, Texas 77546 281-992-3131 281-482-5390 Fax
6 Precedent Drive Rooksley, Milton Keynes MK13 8PR, UK
1385 Woodroffe Av Ottawa, ON K2G 1V8
www.TotalRecallPress.com

Printed in the United States of America with
simultaneously printings in Canada, and
United Kingdom.

1 2 3 4 5 6 7 8 9 10

First Edition

To Patty, Florence, and Malia

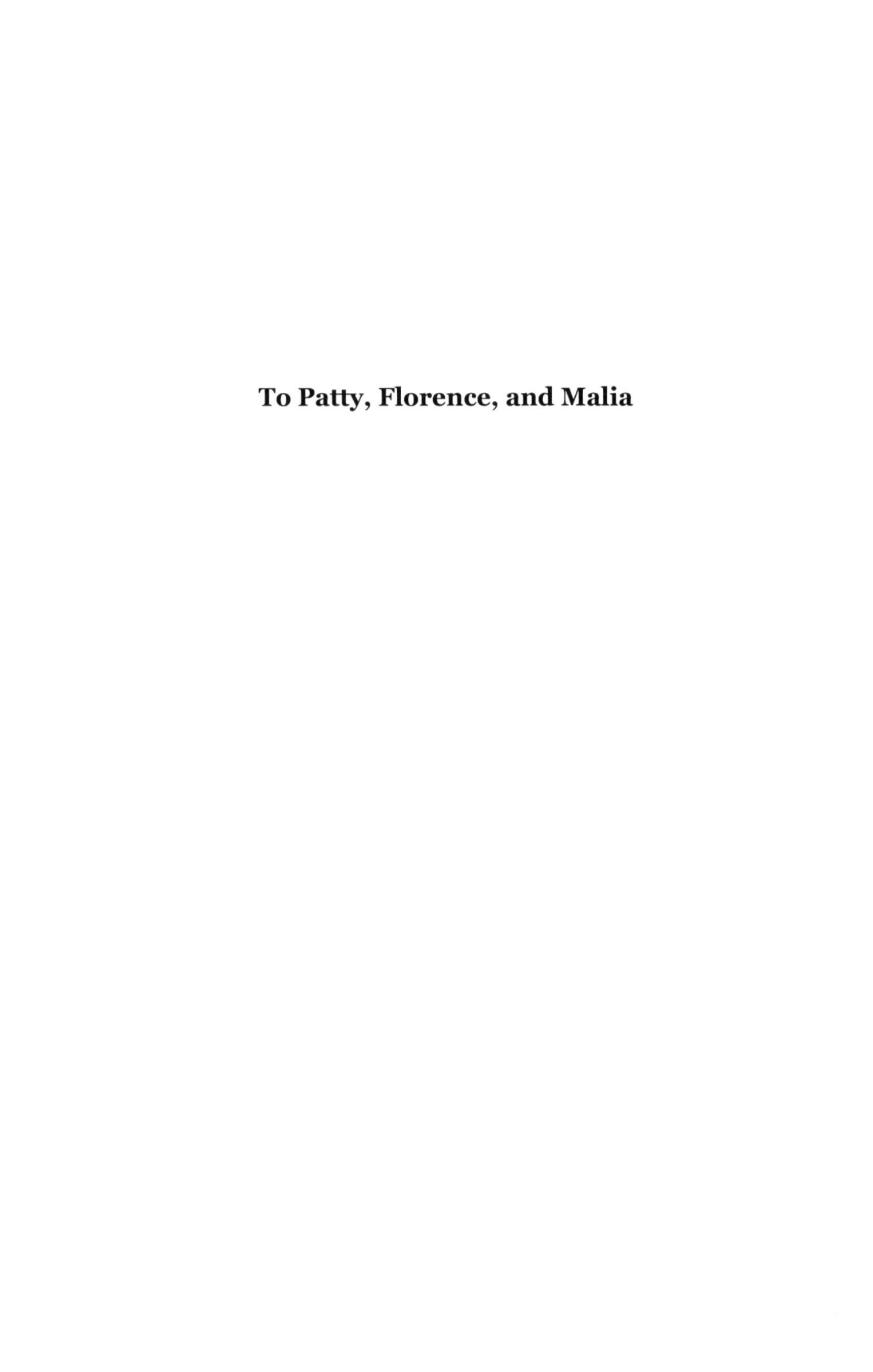

About the Author

Alice Shapiro studied poetry and playwriting briefly with William Packard at New York University. Her poetry has been published in journals and anthologies for 24 years, and a chapbook with Scars Publications "Seasons of the Heart" was published in 2007.

Shapiro's first collection of poems, *Cracked: Timeless Topics of Nature, Courage and Endurance*, was published by TotalRecall Publications (2009) with a preface by Suffolk L.I. Poet Laureate David Axelrod.

She has been nominated for a 2010 Pushcart Prize and a GAYA award (Georgia Author of the Year). A third volume is forthcoming in 2011. Shapiro is also winner of the Bill C. Davis Drama Award for a one-act play (*Four Voices*).

Shapiro currently lives in NW Georgia.

Acknowledgements

Thanks to Gloria Mindock for editing many of these poems, *The Smoking Poet* for publishing "Song," and *Rethink* for the analysis of "Beads."

Table of Contents

DESCENDING » Crimes — 1

- Crime 2
- Beads 3
- Rain 4
- Saved 5
- Homework 6
- Stealing 7
- Bedtime 8
- Noises 9
- Window 10
- Shame 11
- Alive 12
- Change 13
- Germany 14
- If 15
- Quarrel 16
- Cure 17
- Choice 18
- Affair 19
- Tryst 20

DESCENDING » Politics — 21

- Undulations 22
- News 23
- Waiting 24
- Progress? 25
- Politics 26
- Sore 28
- Debt 29

Anxiety 30

　　America 31

　　Layoff 32

　　Christmas 33

　　2009 34

　　Tomorrow 35

DESCENDING » Death　　　　　　　　　　　　　　　37

　　Protection 38

　　Woe 39

　　Dementia 40

　　Child 41

　　Bobby 42

　　Death 43

　　Hovering 44

　　Ambush 45

　　Quiver 46

　　Circle 47

ASCENDING » Nature　　　　　　　　　　　　　　　　49

　　Dawn 50

　　Physics 51

　　Flower 52

　　Change 54

　　Waters 55

　　Maybe 56

　　Rest 57

　　Weed? 58

　　Sand 59

　　Snow 60

　　Fire 61

　　Natural 62

ASCENDING » Ephemera   63

- Relocating 64
- Windows 65
- Interruption 66
- Can't 68
- Think 69
- Future 70
- Business 71
- Return 72
- Wealth 74
- Blackout 75
- Revelation 76
- Apartment 77
- Patty 78
- Break 79
- Midnight 80
- Containment 81
- Museum 82
- Mother 83
- College 84
- Lindy 85
- Manhattan 86
- Neighbor 87
- Journey 88
- Holiday 89
- H-O-M-E 90
- Mattress 91
- Evolution 92

ASCENDING » Creativity — 93

- Fame — 94
- Faded — 95
- Georgia — 96
- Hope — 97
- Illustration — 98

ASCENDING » Love — 101

- Alone? — 102
- Force — 103
- Passion — 104
- Retrospective — 105
- Dreaming — 106
- Almost — 107
- Freedom — 108
- Union — 109
- Glow — 110
- Song — 111

FOREWORD

I was quite honored when Alice Shapiro asked me to write this introduction. We share an artistic passion for life and I love taking voyages with her.

She opens with these words:
Old songs pull us back
and inconsistencies surrender
until we are one with lost scents
and odd paraphernalia.

Now we are home. Let's run down those well-worn paths of memory, the ring of friend's laughter in our ears, the sunny days of old blinding our mind's eye. Wait, not too fast. We might fall and skin a knee, bruise our soul. "Old minds eating brightness / peer back in time..." But do they see?

For this is a darkened home and a bit apprehensive this return -- perhaps our old childhood home has changed, either abandoned since we moved on or occupied now by strangers, and we find the pool out back a brackish portal. Memories a-swirl, emotions a-tumble, new visions are storming in to cloud the mirrored pool of experience.

There is a dark undercurrent in this work which may surprise some readers. It seems incongruous to warn of beauty, as these words are deceptively sumptuous and the manner kind. Pretty does not mean shallow and here we're rapidly moving out into the depths. Darkness is more alive, more filled, more mysterious. I was reminded of Alice's spiderish warning in her book *Cracked*: "For all we learn of weaving, we're / caught in labyrinths / we did not contemplate."

Be amazed at the sunken maze we are entering. In this new volume, she goes on to ask, "Why pierce a wound? / Childhood must keep its sacredness...."

This is the heart of the matter. You find here a quest, a revelation, a piercing of the veil. It may not be as easy as expected, but Alice Shapiro has a very gentle way of leading us into it, of comforting us as we stumble. A bit of mythic thread goes a long way. More than a simple wordsmith, she is compassionate and understands what the human heart feels, needs, bleeds. This inner journey will occur. Luckily we have such a companion to guide us, shield us, push us.

Let us dive deep. What treasures shall we undercover? Ah, tsk, tsk. Your impatience is showing.

Ahead of all games, it is a wonderment
that a cache of jewels is not the prize.

Wild swain had first to gather them intact
from the deep, where an ink-black ocean
conceals a mystery: that one would not survive
the catch. Tangled in sea's rockweed is more
than an occupation. It is the trap.

Don't get trapped. Solving the mystery is the key. The journey is the goal. No one promised an easy ride. Besides, there might just be a monster hiding in our labyrinth. So go slow, explore, discover. No worries, though. Rugged adventure with an ever-present tang of danger in the air is so much more fun than the unexamined.

Now, revel in "the art of darkness" "glow-ing / from the inside."

Thomas Fortenberry
Charlotte, NC

DESCENDING

» Crimes

Crime

A brush against the past beautifies us
revisiting youth, correcting misconceptions
built years upon years of vanity.
Old songs pull us back
and inconsistencies surrender
until we are one with lost scents
and odd paraphernalia.
Seldom still a criminal act
leaks into awareness because suppressed
it is harmless. Why pierce a wound?
Childhood must keep its sacredness
if even theft looms irregular
across a hesitant brow.
It can be cleansing, though, this retreat into pitch-dark
cobweb-rich corners
like a robin's splash in a cloudy street puddle.

Beads

Ahead of all games, it is a wonderment
that a cache of jewels is not the prize.
Pearls laid round a silken neck
contain a power, erect as a queen's dignity,
delicate as a flower in bud. They speak
invisible gossips, judging this and that.
One brushes a hand gently over their roundness
and feels sublime exhilaration, comparing
their company to the ascent of the sun.
Wild swain had first to gather them intact
from the deep, where an ink-black ocean
conceals a mystery: that one would not survive
the catch. Tangled in sea's rockweed is more
than an occupation. It is the trap.

Rain

Cherishing the subtlety of rain,
the culpability of a plump cumulus
strolling across the skyscape,
he champions the dawn, eradicating
doubt, fear, fury.
In a reach for ways out,
he hunches over a yellowed book,
nicked pages symbols of over-use
and reads with silent lips.
Still as sleep, he barely breathes,
attentive for a whisper in the air
to guide, caress him with an answer.
It comes, first faint like raindrops
then pulsing like an aching pain.
Dust scatters at his feet, disturbed by movement
as he scoops the gun from its rusty rack.
Anointed by an ill wind that lied
into his searching ears, and warped
by a will too strong, the voices screeched
relentlessly until a shot was heard.
Rain drizzles over a huddled mass.

Saved

A slow slinky feeling urged its way
through the skinniest veins imaginable
until all were full, bursting
with rage. It only took a moment.
Weeks of calm temper suddenly ended,
paranoia, speed, because a broken promise
passed from lying lips.
It struck me silent for a deathly moment
a foolish frozen smile, sideways eyes
stuck on hate. Stomach bile bubbling.
That was the time to halt, turn around,
breathe deep, sit down, lie down, sleep,
envision deceit as cotton candy
dissolving on a child's tongue.
It was not easy turning lies to mush
and I struggled with conscience and revenge.
If not for the knowledge of higher reciprocal things
there might be a sticky pool of dizzying self-indulgence
and a mind exiled from its mental country.

Homework

Almost done.
Then some children gather on the lawn.
A misty fog descends,
clothes their limbs
with a wet, filmy haze.
One swipes his finger on a water glass
in the shape of a heart.
Laughing, dancing on the spongy earth
they don't bother with the interruption
but I, having turned toward their play
grow fonder of the spectacle
than to writing.
The half-blank page
suffers from imbalance
like standing only on one leg.
With a fleeting, bitter breath
I reclaim my place and place the pen
at the fragmented thought
and set to fancily embroider, embellish it.
A cat's meow and pounce
at a great invisible phantom
takes me, smiling, off the path again.
Incomplete and disillusioned
the lesson has no end.

Stealing

Inspired by a trail
of penned offerings
a lady follows,
snatching at the crumbs of genius
gifted to them.
She recognizes beauty
by its glow, by a mystic
knowing
and scribbles after them
like a bird imitates its mother's flight
as a bee feasting in a flower patch
prying out many mouthfuls.
Soon, she calls upon that hoarded cache
and her repertoire responds.
On a page a mighty thought –
built upon those juxtaposed, fragmented parts
becomes her mark.
It is fact.

Bedtime

A little tea, a little chocolate
late
equalizes, stills
almost like an Adirondack vista seen
from a jutted, perilous perch
on a craggy overhang
peering down miles and miles.

Mindful of the time
it is tiny pleasures
we prolong
that keep us from our bed
cramming in as much folly as
can be stolen,
drawn away from Death's entreaty.

One more hour
one more sip and bite
the lovely power of our palate
the might of a wayward tongue.

Noises

Whoosh.
Tires spin over asphalt
spitting stones
gutter-bound
that join a white, plastic coffee cup
on silken grassy ground.

Screech
into a gravelly driveway.
Brakes skid,
halt before a prostrate bike
left abandoned,
a premonition that inclines
towards tribal ties disbanded.

Oomph.
Gymnasium grunts,
hints of brute and brawn
developing physique to tempt,
charm a woman's casting off garments
made to make us feel un-alone.

Window

1.

Child in a darkened room sees gray
through a window straining eyes
perceiving the wood like a postcard.
Faraway it is like mist and smoke
and a boy's choir. The lad who sinned
runs through a wheat field
trampling golden stalks, out of breath.
He falls naked and looks
into a sea of faces who peer back.
Forgiveness is the course.
If this had been the general sense
of childhood, would not our life be wise?

2.

To what purpose do I roam these walls
pacing and humming fancy melodies
while business bustles this holiday?
It is the end of hurricane season,
the end of detours, and the end of us.
Never a window opened, except now
late into the night when windows
are superfluous because it is dark.
From the grave an echo stabs,
years traveled have no meaning
and confessions occur in the void.
I was pleased and despondent,
woeful and full of glee
when we parted friends.
Today your truth is my oblivion.

Shame

A precious outlawed ivory tusk --
sleek, white-blonde,
severed, polished, sold
to lie prone atop an aged, scored and flecked
mahogany escritoire.
It is a quiet desk
stately, like the once-grand appendage
resting near pens and paper clips
that boasts of ownership—
not as from true origins
once piercing air with pride,
magnificence --
but conceit
a capturing of false bravado
as if one trudged the wild jungles
slayed, and claimed the beast oneself.
Instead it is a furtive money-changing roguery.

A grey, mammoth, hard-rind, wrinkled beast
swaggers as far as possible
confined by iron-barred fetters at the Bronx Zoo
as goggle-eyed babes drool ice cream cones
on bib-less t-shirts
oblivious to a pachyderm's silent cry
out of habitat
out of sensible mind
and, of course, minus weaponry.

Alive

Succulent sweet grape
sip its essence
a balm for the gut
slight shriveling of clarity
tingling tongue
loosed tongue.

From a mountain vista
nudged carefully into a crook
of sun-warmed rocks
I grasped my knees
looked down upon rippling blue waters,
sucked in an orgy of crisp, cool air.

A passionate life
sunk in drink
and a drunken view of nature
share common roots
like twin children
from one fertile womb.

Change

Every day, every footstep
travels in the same groove
from mailbox down tar to Highway 5.
Ritual meanderings past tree and bush
and bark mulch strewn to hinder weeds.
Nothing like confronting New York concrete
wending through a flood of bodies,
slogging swiftly from one peculiar block
with its spicy Asian smells
to yet another clump of high-rise condos
odorless, prim, reluctant.
Endless waves of horns
psychedelic stares from the millions,
wild never-ending change.
Nothing like the waft of fresh-mowed grass
the sweep of tame, blue sky
and the fine, subtle nuance
of Georgia.

Germany

Books are piling up, overflowing shelves
voracious thirst for other's doubt,
transformation, mending.
Music scatters airwaves to flow straight
to swayable ears, serenely accepting
the jazz of it, the drift.
Meanwhile Baden-Baden's roulette wheels
spiced an evening,
and plush carpet silenced reason.
That was then,
pretending we could slide unannounced
through royalty, like gods drunk on fake celebrity.
It is a drip from a faucet
interrupting a lonely night dressed with
half-read volumes and honky-tonk.
Sweet sentiments, dead-quiet room
mixed like a good cocktail in a trembling hand.

If

If, after a length of time
nothing changes
try to erase childhood.
When waiting is not enough
wait longer
until you see the cusp of death.
Divine images in a frothy cloud
spying down on two old souls
will rain an urgent welcome.

If a faultless lover fades to black
and you trudge a cobblestoned alley
alone, all pictures in your mind
dissolved like pink carnival candy,
try building a new nation.
When sparks jump off concrete walls,
inevitable resistance to change,
down a sweet Brown Betty.
Many husbands, under oaths, have warmed
to pretty perfidy.
After years nestled in wondering,
try spreading innocence.

Quarrel

Among the ashes, brute force crushed
small flakes of black, the soot
sticking to a boot heel, and he cried.
Laid down in the muck, tucked in a corner
a velvety scarf, torn from a sleek neck
ends its enthusiasm on a dismal night.
The fight, a crescendo from tiny swipes
at vulnerabilities, like all
such troubles, took half a day.
Light failed slowly in the anteroom
as afternoon slipped gently into twilight
and where a last attempt to reconcile
fell on a stampede of screams.
Halt. Harrowing spats like this
leave no easy exits,
like a California obsession with the act,
and both tears and wearied arguments
lose their salt.

Cure

Habit, tricking the nerves, strings her out.
Twitches, tics and rolling eyes vex
while stretched limbs reach toward heaven.
A guttural scream scares even the owls
and jackals skulking in a dark forest.
Drink deep from a fountain of dreams
when days were carefree and wildflowers, dripped
with dew, gently swayed in the wind.
Take this vision all the way to relief, to pause
from pain. Meditate on eradication, death.
Prevent a clawing at bed sheets by sheer will.
Wait patiently as Hell vanishes and tears dry.
Miraculous peace appears at the eleventh hour.

Choice

In the jumble of thoughts that ring through the day
it is expected that one should arise and solidify,
be the impetus for action, the cause and credibility.
Activator of the past, a fragment loosens, is set free.
Whiffs of chocolate can carry heavy loads, sweeten
unbearable tasks with their honey and silk.
Soldier's gift to the waif running shoeless in the dirt.
Pacifier of all vulgarity, lifter of foul inclinations,
tender-hearted men call it flirtation.
Stout bellies and plump hands grovel for its flavor.
It is the end all of distress, and champion of distraction.
Reverting to one's thoughts is anathema, the curse
when chocolate is consumed both by mouth and memory.
Fear devours the appetite for choice, as we prefer
procrastination and to lick our fingers free from thought.

Affair

Children stare, open-mouthed at that which makes no sense,
sway in place as if a jarring poke at space might betray it.
A simple act of washing clothes is erudite
combined with quips from memories.
I wash and wash and still stains embed themselves
in delicate fabrics, in strange recesses of a brain
that selects randomly when I am looking elsewhere.
If written down, the gap between then and now
shrinks like cashmere in hot water.
Ruminating on past dirt I am cleansed of guilt.
Sins of omission keep up a façade
that children recognize as dual. It is in this
questionable atmosphere that soiled laundry collects.
And fresh, clean clothes absolve secret indiscretions.

Tryst

Before the law, is the cesspool,
a whirlwind or a tempest,
cutting and shaping character
like a sculptor's chisel at marble.
Sweat beads on a creased brow,
a lone tear squeezes from eye's edge,
down-turned lips, ruby red and swollen
barely mouth syllables of regret
before we reach the ultimate embrace.
It is in desire that two bodies fuse,
two night-chameleons, soul-exploiters,
rocking to the rhythm of crickets and toads.
Relinquish that old grasp on always,
touch all manner of tenderness.

DESCENDING

» Politics

Undulations

Ha! The news is worse than eye allergies
in the midst of golden pollen season.
News is burned into a stream of thoughts
quiet and deep until some cancer topples life.

Waking now in a gratitude mode
I veer away from trans fats, salt
and second-hand smoke.
Breakfast on the porch my father built,
acacias listing from an eastern wind,
it seems late to change a favorite ritual
of chocolate sauce drizzled
over French vanilla ice cream.
This, however, makes more sense than hate.

I rose early today, waited with patience
as the world crept crooked, bumping
into bombs blasting the guts out of
cars and children, tiny souls of sorrow.
I waited longer for a spark
until a fisherman sunk his line
and the placid shining lake rippled.

News

Is it criminal
to sit on one's haunches
while the nation cries?
Soldiers die.
Inept correctness desecrates
their graves.

"Silver now prohibited
for China's multitude"
is the new announcement.
We are rising to their level
as our rulers rule
unconcerned about our frowns.

I use my ears like antennae
breathing to the bongo beat
that advertises tropical fruit
on TV.

I have called before
expressed my view,
outraged they consider me
inept.

Laws are passed regardless,
and my drift
to sit again and suck myself
out of consciousness
wins.

Waiting

Faced with options,
I cannot choose
easily
from the chaos
of excess.
Rather, Sweden's sun reflects
off spare, white walls, built-in closets.
It is crisp and ornament free.
Their focus lies elsewhere,
somewhere in the realm of sport.
Dare I gather more
while the multitude drops
to its material knees?
Having had the cold displeasure
of lack
I weigh tenuously
a tactful stab at opulence.
What is mine will come to me.

Progress?

An old man who calls himself bum
turns out wiser than judges.
He gazes at the ceiling
as snow slithers down the station-wagon window
that substitutes for home
as the half-frozen pond crackles
from a northern wind.
In his dreams he drives
along a green-edged highway,
sunny palms passing on the periphery
no longer saddled by circumstance.

Into Spring things correct
like the peep of a budding hydrangea
after its cold hiatus,
a door ajar, inviting
and he leapt at it,
his visionary summer trek pushed back
into a distant recess,
his alternate lifestyle squeezed further
into oblivion
as he suited up and bussed
along city streets
to a glass architectural wonder
where he could watch snow
slide down its extravagantly windowed face.

Politics

They argue
two peculiar points of view
passionate and certain
of facts, benefits, truth.
Their confidence sways
and heads turn left, right, center,
RIGHT, CENTER, LEFT
until our mouths gape open
while we beg for a trickle
of wisdom to drip downward
onto our outstretched tongues
like a stranded Bedouin
crawling the sands of Gobi
delirious, parched.
Sprung from founders
who organized
our even path,
we've tried tricks and loopholes
to amass private pockets
full and overflowing.
Faced now by gangster blueprints
taking speech under a restrictive wing
we wake from dazed pleasantries,
line up for unemployment cash, our ration
of health and fruit.

Looking sideways served no one
but no one will forgive our fault
as they push
to rule unruly
stupid mobs.

Sore

The pain on my skin
settles scattered thoughts
taking distractions to task
as I focus on one critical spot.

A child's bandage could not soothe
nor mother's kiss erase distress,
wipe brutal torment off,
a sure test of tolerance.

Here, life's drama dawns again
trickling in on all fours
but trying to forget is futile, feckless
and the hurt regains its dominance.

My good friend suffers, her burden
a millstone, constant and unchecked.
I think of her always bent and aching.
It lifts me from self-pity
as my facile hand grazes over
the throbbing war wound.

Debt

Then, a tedious cloud pressed down hard
on her id
like hot irons frying silk.
Deep, linty pockets, drained, empty-cashed,
grew bigger, and bigger with interest.
Usury, usury.

For fifteen dark, judged winters
several thousands owed to the man
laid heavy like wet wadded paper
in her hand.

Then, ignorant of fate
she saw the debt come down.
She thanked the tanked economy,
kissed the ground
that now sustained her ego.

Anxiety

Farm boys barefoot in the chicken coop
peer outward at a brilliant sunrise
hens squawking, pecking at his thrust hand
stealing their unborn young.
Did you ever feel a nappy carpet
brush mild against a shoeless foot?
It is comfort plain and simple
and so easy to miss.
A sun at eight has no feature.
It is hidden in a common brightness.
Unremarkable day begins.
Which poison do you swallow first --
tap water leached with toxins, metals, dirt
perhaps a cup of joe, its caffeine revving
up retarded limbs asleep with sleep?
Go forward world, your toys adept
at bringing leisure, and wave goodbye
to ease.

America

America, birth land of a small girl
surrounded by strange ephemera,
slumping dogs sniffing trash,
half-smoked butts in city gutters,
fallen soldiers, coke and fries.
I hear a foreign tongue from Farsi mouths,
Hindi tunes, Nuyorican poets
while I walk
through ever-changing zones.
America, mountain and dry plain,
host immaculate, lovely quest
take me straight to failure's end.
Each tryst, a hint of something rare,
perfume of a sultry eve, a cried-on shoulder
where a soul felt crushed one lonely instant.
Redemption easy with a glimpse of simple grandeur
held tightly in its palms and firs
and oceans lit by a low-hung moon.

Layoff

Justice for the weary wage earner
while a lover of cash gathers sums
upon sums, is begged beyond endurance.
Files of men, pink-slipped, wait in line
for pretty pennies to stuff their pockets,
eyes upset by worry and a mix of pride.

He stares unfocused, sighs drifting from
his slight bent shoulder, a sob caught
between a throat's swallow and the air.
Where is the paisley dress for his child
whose liberty depends on peers?

Draped on a steel mannequin
the cloth almost shines
and the child salivates at the promise.
He holds onto delicate fingers
and pulls, and breaks the spell.

Christmas

Broken and exhausted with no fight left
news of danger, damage, woe
seeps in, skulking to an unemployed few.
On the periphery, a bland hope
trickles into a half-shut embrace.
The race is taken up also as it was before
to the we that once scuttled the treadmill.
And there goes time in the uneasy efforts
that used to choke creativity. Jammed up,
inventions of imagination fall, sink, die.

It is a season demanding joy, as if chaos
was invisible and the muddle unfamiliar.
White snow, supposed to soothe,
drifts dirty, and city streets soon disturb.
We advance incrementally
as foreclosure waits until Spring so waifs
in fleece pajamas can see St. Nick.
Warm by the fire, the world shrinks
and half-way round the globe where children cry
gets so close it is heard within our own adventure.

2009

Of all the years the world has cried
this one is marked with promise.
At other times, knees scraped and scratched,
some bent, kneeling,
have found their mutual pain to be
muddled with equal filth.
And it grew fatter as days passed,
fat with greed, stuffed full.

Change has come.
At the renaissance we now have hope
as our belts are tightened
and the frightened mass is rumbling,
even stumbling, with its fragile steps
toward betterment, a kind of joy
returning to a pioneer spirit.

Tomorrow

Push. Emphasize. End—
for this is the nation of possibility.
Any brilliant task will do
what the mob fails to recognize
in its frenzied apathy.
Think of New Year's Eve, crowded
streets of huddled, bundled, raving
celebrations
while a narrow alley breaks the back
of sleazy calculations
to rob, to distribute contraband.
The underworld beyond the cheers
is lit by an exploding sky.
Glad shouts rise for tomorrow
beyond the damp, ratty lane,
neither dark nor light,
both tense at the eclipse of choice.

DESCENDING

» Death

Protection

Slow death, years
dying, decay
and then a pasty clay-face,
clown-features stretched over still bones
peering at a high-vaulted ceiling
nothing else
penetrates even to the core.
Dust will settle eventually
into the cold, hard earth
and a final merging
no difference
between the flame and its heat.

Lilac bushes lined the yard
giant sweetness of air
blown wherever from windy summers.
So alone, a child of nature
nothing else.
But backlands are not the house
where young mother glides
between stove and humid laundry room,
the fangs of death still distant.
Remember this
keep a purple vision safe.

Woe

Cellar sludge, a brownish hue
clogs the habits of convenience.
Two feet, six feet
water climbs and covers,
debris is caught in the raging stream
that cuts a road, halved
to flow its course, washing
loose the woman clinging.

The flood has soaked a book.
Sideways in the midst of waist-high water
a warped desk floats in a once-used room
of cloistered comfort.
A child's doll, fat from moisture
escapes its crib and bumps and bumps
the plaster crumbling,
drowns in filth.

Dementia

The great phrase that jumped
out of a half-listening brain
has escaped
cannot be found
either in the atmosphere
or on the tongue's tip.
Days pass searching for it
like lost car keys
or mother's secret admonition
there, but not there.

Into afternoon it fades
like a waning sun
from pink to deep, deep violet,
like the ocean's floor
muffled, dissolving like wetted salt.
No more.
Weep and mourn for this lost promise—
an atom-child shed like dead skin.
This one—
the future?

Child

When I married Henry
and a child filled the womb
a restless song mutated to a filmy gloom
like shifting tectonic plates
like urging onion-tears to stiffen
for no reason.

Predestined for the tomb
the little package slipped
from one old world through this portal
only left to lie, satin shrouded
in the bosom of clouds
cloudy mission
clouded eyelids, speech, lineage.

Our hearts fell flat
pumped out of love
primed for abstinence.
In a twinkling slip
a seeding
and the ache budded
into innocence, the son,
immortality overdue, a grin.

Bobby

What sense makes a primate know
just how to peel its fruit,
a fledgling bird to flap tiny wings
or you to love me?

I think it was death.

Good mourners filed quietly
into a crushed velvet room
all purple as dense drapery.
A mother's tears the host,
the dreadful center of attention.
All drawn, pallid faces glanced
sidelong at her,
feet shuffling, the only sound
that mattered
while her son's spirit ascended.

I think it was a bond.

What better ointment
poured over a sorrow
than love.

Death

Scratch away brown, crusty scars,
protections covering a bruise.
Kiss the healing air, it is cleansing.
And mother's breath soothes a child's horror
when moonlight casts its doom-shadows.
My tears failed her.

Tricks on handlebars to claim applause
from a distant man
went almost missing.
It was not surprising that
joy caught me up at his final parting.

Still, bound by invisible affection,
I have not cut the cord
and therefore do not meet the world.
No reason for a cry when they have not departed
yet sadly it is complete that I touch nothing.

Hovering

Hovering, treading time in layers
we sit silently on a cliff, meadow grass
below and look backward. An old woman
nods off, her wrinkled arm leaning
coldly on a park bench, the sun fading
like memories which formed her outlook.
We laughed while dancing round
her sleeping body, deaf to jays and canines.
An absence, an abundant hush
returned as we recognized the stealth,
the skulking promise of an aged future
and looking deep into our eyes, brittle truth was hard.
Bones, bones, fragile frame that turns to dust,
eighty years to our twenty, must we have this?
Days feel easy, embraced by trust
and we reject all fellowship with senility.

Ambush

Hound at his master's feet, docile, petable,
shifts fiercely, reverting to his carnal instinct
as he is rousted to ire. His jaw, galvanized,
grips an intruder's arm refusing to abandon it.
At odds with a lion, who tears at his prey,
this beast fastens on and clamps down.

Cur at birth is all soft fur,
summoning up the hardest heart to warm.

Carnivore matures with kindhearted discipline.
It is strange how man commands such nature,
governing it as if it were a child.
Cognizing nuances of language and spirit,
dog pacifies himself second in command,
except in rowdy moments when original disposition
halts all training and to the contrary, kills.

Quiver

A tall emaciated tree
deep within a forest
embellished by
an eye-shaped knob
leaking sap from its corner
called up great sadness.
Leaves shook eerily
until no one dared remain
in the macabre edge of doom.

In a quiet day or two
when least alert
tumult, rancor, ache
and limbs interlaced with rubble,
a quake's ten thousand souls.
Buried neath the trembling dust
silence only, and wailing.

That was then, when days were black
now light pervades deep sleep.
Raised from soot and ashes
one foot advances, and another.
A mangy shell of man survives
to spin and grow illuminated,
backward from the red, red rage.

Circle

At four I saw Daddy's tears
through a window
from the whitest room,
cold, strict, tainted.
It was neutral to me,
and puzzling.

At seven I saw Daddy's tears
when Grandmother abandoned earth
and changed to dust.
Thin, baby arms wrapped his shoulder
with new-known depth.
Self and other touched,
roles reversed.

At forty-seven I saw Daddy's breath
fill another white, chilled space
with heavy sounds
and a heaving death-rattle.
As he passed into a new dimension
I saw joy, lightness,
dry-eyed freedom.

ASCENTING

» Nature

Dawn

Light and light even into corners
upon the dredge and silt
lying heavy on our path
like a felled tree from a lightning strike.

Stand steady as we explore this past.
Release the hold a deep hurt has
watch the dove take it high
and it falls into the sea like rain.

Good, bright dawn, your voice ensures
no pity, no jazz, no drool.
Cut to bits, the damage fades as mist
and the shine is evermore.

Physics

Twin mountains, purple, hazed
bring an easy sleep
as they scatter big sounds
like seed broadcast in a strong wind
and the flatlands ooze a hush
being softened by the sun's heat.
Beyond idyllic pasture
a dark nation under blades of grass
festers, bustles, wars.
Alone in its dimension
of snake, insect, worm
it is ignorant of death's footstep
that romps the surface with joy.
This view of two peculiar worlds
seldom meets at the same spot
except on God's watch,
and idle contemplation.

Flower

1.

A lone fake flower absent a name
not a dahlia, chrysanthemum, nor wildflower
is adrift in a waterless jar
dry as winter, forlorn as a soldier's wife
who is lost to the desert where dust
hardly settles. Her eyes, specked
with tears, overlook the bud,
a permanent accessory wedged below petals
made of silk. In fuchsia and baby pink,
stamen sculpted by human effort
have long histories, unlike a natural blossom
that rises in morning and sees early death.
Devoid of fragility the pretender rose or peony
can only gather household dust, or be tossed aside
on some hill of trash to be forever buried intact.

2.

It is wintry. Walks are not leisurely.
The brush is peripheral, a blur.
If a flower is present there are no eyes
gazing into its empathic elegance.
Haste at the expense of beauty
engages all, even those with predisposition
toward nature's demand. And a silent
reprimand, a call to recognize the past
came fleeting by of moments when we met,
touched, an intimacy now forgotten.

Hesitant to grip that drama once again
eyes fell downward and away
as if in its speed we also did not exist.

3.

The rose of past glimmerings
is different than today's fortune.
What then seemed golden
moved so quick and caught
its wings in the net of mortality.
Now we talk, share rare moments
that death has ruined.
It is too late.
Our time flowered, amassed its destiny.
Bouquets of roses cannot defend what's gone
nor dispel the sadness of love.

Change

Here in this narrow attitude
not much is promised.
It is hard to walk, room to room,
focus strained and pointed at the past.
A real look, not at the beating,
but away from the shame of weakness whispers
that useless stacks of repetitious junk
fail to satisfy.
Fade out, fade in, fade to black.

Here at sunrise attainment is
the greatest possible future.
Shed horrors with outstretched ghostly arms
have no sway this new amazing day.
Their cries dissolve like magic tricks
or ice melting into water.
Lazy walks mature into vast mercurial awakenings
where chrysanthemums burst open
and a fresh grass incense dusts the valley.

Waters

Two totally bluish water basins
intersect at Wesley Pond
like a collage painting.
Who maps out the land
wet on wet?
It is confusing
as the brain reconciles concrete,
lake.
On closer look, both man-made pools
irritate, raise questions of intent—
how much leisure can be built
into a small acre
of trees mixed with asphalt,
a hint of chlorine,
squalid muck near waddling ducks
their webs deep in a rim of silt?

Maybe

No
and endings pop.
No ma'am
Georgia bows to manners
and in the sultry heat deeds die.
How long have voices from mind's pit
broken down a fragile wish?

Behold the feline beast--
dry-mouthed, quiescent, pale
since the kill
set, upon a moment's notice,
to writhe in pleasure
at a friendly stroking.
She cares not for scorn,
leaps high into the sky
to down a lovely butterfly
no shame, no fear.

Take heed to turn a no-phrase
from loss to jubilance
dance barefoot
whiff the cherry-blossoms
yes.

Rest

Barefooted, crushing a summer-scorched lawn
the fair-skinned wanderer witnessed
an academy of waterfowl sliding along Peachtree lake.
Wasps danced with malice in their buzz
and she quit paradise without doubt.
Is it predictable that beauty be threatened by pain?

Multicolored lounge-chairs glistening
with absent bathers' sweat
attract her beat-down bones.
She takes a lazy mid-day sleep,
but wakes abruptly, horror on her dry, parched lips.
A boy with loaded pistol shot an interloper
and slow, the dream dissolves, the guilt remains.
Is it just reproof for stealing time?

From the corner of her eye the wasp returns
claiming broader territory.
Nothing more except retreat,
she fastens on the concept "rest"
from out the shell of cracking circumstance.

Weed?

A yellow dandelion lawn
was wish fulfilling when weeds
morphed into flying diaphanous things
scattered in air
by a child's big breath and a blow.
They eat dandelions now
tossed in arugala salads,
chic green feasting for an upper class.
And in a foreign land the bitter plant
is prized for healing.
Yellow happiness, yellow beauty
ripped by suburban mowers
from their fragile roots and flung
into black plastic sacs to wilt and die.

Sand

A woman and an Old English sheepdog
tumble and leap playfully along the shore
at dusk. Beneath tons of ocean-water
vicious sea animals bottom-feed and copulate.
A clump of sand is stuck
under silken strands of long-flowing hair --
both the beast's and hers. They are friends,
ignorant of danger because they love.

On an abandoned mid-night beach
everything turns black,
slapping waves launch deafening sounds
into an infinite container called sky.

The woman steadies herself gazing at the pitch-dark sea
in a barren-eyed stupor from high on a redwood deck,
love drained,
love lost.
She has replaced it with teardrops.
A lover's absence intrudes on glory.

Snow

I'd forgotten --
flakes drop from above,
blanket an almost-Spring, almost-green turf,
and it is all white.
Soft snow clings to the Bradford Pear,
melts on asphalt.
The South, confused by snow
transforms its sultry reputation
and I am pleasured, being North by birth.

Fire

Autumn, autumn,
down an alder branch
while the black stewpot sways
faintly from the hearth-fires.
She stirs its innards,
fat with guinea fowl,
meat that warms a spreading paunch,
a tune about her beefy lips.
A waft of chicory's promise
fills the homely cabin with its mist.
The eye suggests 1891,
heart of badlands cut from lusty cloth
and Whitman's *Leaves of Grass*,
his eidolons, ever "crumbling,"
a long-forsaken path ever changing.
Today, the chimney, symbol only,
points to progress in that steam arises
up from floorboards and a paper log
flames uniformly, homogenized
and useless. We follow faint blue embers
fading, gripped a moment not by beauty,
nor utility but only sparks of antecedents
that we hope will be enough to quell malaise.

Natural

The geometry of shadows
shaped from natural and manufactured forms,
from trees, and grandfather clocks
in our old English foyer
throw subtle gradient tones
disappearing into light
and decorate the earth.

Leaves tumbled across an asphalt back-lot
bright against black
make a pattern
freeze-frame ripe
for a quick-stolen snapshot.

Seeing
is simple, keen
takes time
like making love
early, easily.

ASCENSING

» Ephemera

Relocating

It's done, with no looking back
moving, as litter blows down Chelsea streets,
grey streets oozing stale milk smells at 5 a.m.
Eerie calm while rats possess the dawn.
How it measures dark against a grass-green suburb.
Yet this sterile, flawless landscape puzzles.
Look further after settling in and find
bland prisons of nullity and void.
Do you know fear? You panic, you die.
It is the way of a city.
But humdrum, bourgeois days produce a resignation
so rest goes on, with only slugs and worms
to fret about. Though urban roads provide no place
for prancing barefoot, what would that prove?
You can't go back to innocence, so move.

Windows

It is the time
fluttering skirts become passive listeners
as they rest on chair cushions
spreading beauty as if Vermeer
were there with brush in hand,
an eye sparkling over taffeta folds,
a heart transferring joy into the future.

We watch the girl peer out a window
like our pensive days, our youth.
What seduces us to face the sun
when all that's seen are ponderings,
the play of mind's redundant reel?

So deep, we sleep in petticoats
and listen to the dust cling to its hosts—
heroic oak armoires, broad bedsides
fitted with silk, brocade footstools
bracing dainty feet.
It is bright, it is crisp and clear-sighted
to that inward scene.

Interruption

It is the deepest part of night.
Resisting the exit from sleep,
eyes swollen shut,
still half within a dream,
Nature calls.
It takes some while
to transition
from sedentary rest
into just enough awareness
to sense the danger of retreat
back to the pillow.
So, the trek begins from bed
in the moonless dark.
A hand extends,
an eye's substitute
to navigate the path ahead—
past armoire
past door jamb
trembling, reaching for
the blinding light.
It is within this faint condition,
business done,
that comes another invitation—
the lure of sinking back to
dark oblivion,
supplanted
by the pen.

Into the unseen dawn,
scratches on a page
recount
a journey won—
one more day on Earth,
one more sun.

Can't

Can't think, can't focus, stress
has beaten down minutia.
What garments, draped and flowing
no longer feel sympathetic
on bare skin because of discrepancies
between a man wrestling with his morals
and a woman treading water?
She matures in an age of technicalities,
moon-shadows cast their blueness
over her quick decisions, and his neck bristles.
She could go on forever, not making sense.
He drops dead at fifty, her world dissolves.
What is on her mind, a mind adrift,
sorrowing? A song trickles through the clouds
its melody sprinkling like a sun shower
deep, tempering sad thoughts.
La, la, it is often given as a salve.

Think

I think, turning sight
inward
that I am whole
then shine a light on thoughts
while trees stop existing.
Concentrating hard
on tasks to do
I ruminate on their completion
and miss the quick gone sunset,
miss the death
of scrambling ants beneath my feet.

What if
what if it ended then
like that
with no more trees
or ants
or cracks between a concrete walk?

Rain falls down.
My face lifts towards the unseen moon.
No one can tell the drops from tears
as outside disappears
and I am left alone with
who I think I am.

Future

Torn by promise that fades
and wide swings of anticipation
it is hard to imagine the future.
If a vision could emerge
from the deep encrusted mound
of rhetoric and good intentions
what cool inventions
could top a man's
surfing on a ring of Saturn?
But the children
prosper
and from their tinkering
the miracles a bell-bottomed, long-haired
ancient sees
amazes the eyes of the elders
who once dreamed dreams
as they floated on the Moon.

Business

Collapsed, cutting off visual focus
staring blankly into air
too tired to think,
the sofa is sanctuary
evicting weeks of pressure
put upon by an ache to thrive.
I've spent effort building up
this project
as if my arms
pulled a breached foal
fighting, from the womb.

In this fake, limp reverie
in the midst of hazy transition
questions on the worth
of having done the deed
arise, taunting, teasing…
"What of outcome?"
Doubt about its value,
wasted hours in gestation
health degenerating
from lack of sleep
gulping meals without digestion
keeping life discrete.

It is kindred to birthing art
which when done
brings order,
and sweat from satisfying work.

Return

The girl wakes early
inches sleep-drenched thighs
over crumpled cotton percale
scratching gently her morning skin.

It is new—
the air and her fresh mind
after an hour or two.

Beauty slips by the girl's cheek
exposed partially to sun.
She fails to notice,
lifts a stack of paper,
begins an accounting.
Maine's grand landscape
and sea
flash by her eyes
halting the tedium
grown accustomed to.

The girl remembers.
She discards a common weakness,
stands, flees fast as
brown skittish rabbits
startled by buckshot.
She returns to the weeping willow
whose tendrils sweep along
summer grass.

The girl respects herself
puts passion ahead
of smoky-voiced objections
that claim doom.

Wealth

The beastie in a grotesque garden
has left his habitation
roaming wildly, seeking substitution
screaming into night, homeless.
He, the now-defunct
puppet master
seems less from this perspective.
I used to give him credence
and peer at him in awe
like a tutor blessed with knowledge
the door to strength and power.
Now he dwindles like a snowflake
melting on warm city streets.
Laugh,
squeeze life until it cries
no more.

Blackout

Inched and inched across the white line
as pouring rain mauled our black acrylic roof,
cars lining up to make a mid-street turn
into the puddle-soaked parking lot just left behind.
Half-way home we reached the stop-light,
paused and sought permission from the green swaying harbinger
and waited innocent of danger.

A crackling flash of white-hot sparks
like fourth of July fireworks
smacked the service station pole, lit the sky.
Lights extinguished, sad stores blackened now.
The house, that comfort, that bastion against hostility
emitted darkness, fear, awe.

Candlelight. My shelter from the storm was bruised
and Whitman, Thoreau, Quakers floated nigh.
This longest hour lacking ease
made a still space, a tiny black hole sucking pep
and a forced quiet, feel endless.
Then softly, without pomp, barely discernable
waves of pleasure.

Revelation

After throwing on a ragged mohair shawl
to keep iced air from blowing emphatically
on my naked summer arms,
a heavy-lidded afternoon called me to sleep.
While away, stunning things arose —
indulgent painless dancing
on clouded puffs of eggshell white,
whiffs of lavender, patchouli, sage,
Moorish doors, railings filigreed in a Rodinesque yard
and symphony eyes drinking in an old red velvet opera house.

After several hours, eyes peeped at walls
blank, devoid of image, starkly solid.
Had I hope of foreign films flickering
suddenly on this perfect screen
we could leave satisfied all was well.
But no, no second chance at dreams.
Dragging feet, I scuffed the cool linoleum
saved only by the wisp of light that blinded,
like lightning, or a flashing camera. It struck the retina,
a death-moment that cured an immature cancer.

Apartment

Onion smells ooze out the bathroom vent;
the upstairs tenant cooks late at night
while I try to see without glasses.
It is nobler at life's last quarter
to seek cures
to remedy old age by denial
thus this try at vision's mend.
What is left for a simple recluse,
prisoner of four cramped walls,
except entertainment for a voyeur
eyeing van Gogh prints, an O'Keefe calendar,
carpet stains, and budding branches
out a curtained window?
So narrow like a tunnel
and only one voice echoes in it.
It is known that Bonsai trees
flourish staying small.
What better atmosphere for a mortal
to sniff stale dust
and maybe the cinnamon bun that numbs?

Patty

Though blurred and indistinct
there was a time two sisters
roamed throughout childhood, pals,
funky allies
on shopping sprees to Hempstead
magic ice cream soda, bus-ride world.
Sisters, born into a strange clan
of drunkenness and crossword puzzles
cruise together now at sunset
on the road to mental health,
one's kindness-halo beaming.

Break

Inside a foggy head, the TV talks
instructions spewed from radio waves.
Rusty iron bars shield lunatics
from summer rains, electric shocks, and screams.
It is hard to crawl below these rigid masks
fastened to fear, rage, mystification
and sail into a bright place where joy
sits in the pit of a heart.
And then they drag his lazy feet
into a dark mahogany room
where a shadowy man speaks.
"Talk to me" he quips
as if cathartic words will smooth an ache
lodged securely in a secret chasm.
Bitter mind rules, unleashed upon itself
and simple kicks fail to flourish.
And the hours pass.
Soon, fragrant dogwood seeps
into the tiniest vigilance.
Hope again exists,
and there within ashes rises balance.

Midnight

At midnight as I wake from dreams,
horrors that encumber peace,
distant roars from racing cars emerge
from out the stillness, and pull, thankfully,
at my attention.
Where are the chirping birds, familiar sounds
to recognize its morning? No sun, and so
it is time to turn to darkness and the bed
again. Recoiling from the tasteless prospect,
water splashed on bleary eyes,
I trudge toward waking fully and sit erect.
Deep inside, and still asleep, a portion of me balks
at midnight that to start a day is futile.
A tragic fear pours its message down into
the light, and resistance owns the night.
I fight it. I reason, pledge to try
all the while staring at a blackness
that beckons plain to weariness.
Lost between two worlds, I think.

Containment

Fire-glazed porcelains line a wooden bench,
trembling from a slight breeze.
The barn, stale and sour
offers secrets held tight for decades
and these pretty pots almost wipe
the hidden clean with their
distraction. Buried below, beneath
smiles and pride of artistry, scratching to get out,
the innocent night falls permanently and hard.
Turn away, search out a beautiful curve,
rich patina or a delicate crackle
in the skin of a slender vase. Think not
about his breath, his passion deep into morning.

It is a simple glint in the eye of the lost,
the ones who walk with lowered head
desperately seeking a vital but unattainable past
that conjures up an object craved,
not only remembered. And I want.
Not only vessels to sate the eye
but scattered fragments merging,
liberating an old escapade.

Museum

Talk, hollow in high-ceilinged rooms
drifts unclear and stays background noise.
Art watchers stroll hallways into a maze
of spaces studded with color, line, sentiment.
It is holy, a point where crimson brushstrokes
unseat a bad economy and fierce quarrels
from last night's doleful tragedy.
Into canvas, one disappears from rain,
time, purpose as if flying off to Neverland.
On Mondays, when doors are closed
you can hear your own footsteps clacking
over marble floors, the stone-cold rising
but not disturbing eyes planted
fast onto painted boards, silent gallant stories,
captured fables of cornfields, satyrs, sunflowers.
That year, spent stealing time with culture
was fine, the masters curing any melancholy
in flight across a furrowed brow.
Now, smack in front of failing eyes
an intimate enclave, host and sustainer,
rebirths beauty on a static blue screen.
In private, a heart ascends again.

Mother

The wave hugs a sandy shore
retreating back to its wet mother,
not flooding the gates of bungalow row.
A mongrel stray swaggering along a wind-swept
dune, yelps loudly to the moon.
Mysterious sea, black sea, comfort
sounds wrapped in memory bundles,
cold, then warm, startle me.
From trance one can wake abruptly.

Asleep in the corner of a couch
Chopin's subtle rhythms seeping into rested ears,
a child recalls a mother's gift
as she plays an old piano.
This ancient music stays
a repertoire, a patch of sunlight
through years and years, tears.
Standing shallow in the salty brine
listening to the ebb and flow,
a mother's hands whisper from the deep.

College

As a dark room throbbed with sound
emerging from a big, black box,
indulgence in the wee morning light
became the crowd's theme.
They jumped, writhed, hollered loud.
In the darkness, sweat beaded up
on dancing torso's and palms holding palms.
Too much gin and a waft of liquor smell,
tobacco mixed with body heat, a hell
that's spinning a drunken atmosphere.
I do not long for you.
That whisper teasing, begging more,
I toss you over, stomp upon your plea.
And I am settled on this couch,
this floor of solid oak, alert to sounds
filtering in from dogwoods listing,
bees busy on my green, green grass.

Lindy

Push a boundary, smear a tear
with the back of your hand.
Paint your eyelids with an iridescent hue.
Plastic face, brand new and smiling.
Once, blue taffeta swished along the floor
while we swayed, our high school hearts
fluttering as if we had answers.
It was not exactly right, the surface
smooth but beneath a lie.
Peering at the mirror, pale lips
turn crimson with a sweep of color.
Is it then, or is it now?

Manhattan

I cannot spend the length of days
staring out my window spying
dirty boys in a hot street playing,
sun sparkling off the water
spewing from the open faucet
of a hydrant split from its rusted rest,
their tiny feet immersed in puddles
rife with silt and broken glass
while a stray brown bitch barks.
I close old eyes and in a dream shimmy
down the metal stairs leading to their heaven,
join them in their flaming dance,
being once again as seven years.
Night draws near and distant mother-voices call.
One by one the crowd disperses to a dinner table
and there I lay (and there I be from higher vision)
as warmth passes from a senile brain and blue, blue veins.

Neighbor

Calling your name,
delight is hidden from my night visions,
dreams. The whisper skips
over a scarlet-hued horizon
where an arm's embrace has disarmed
everything. It is only remembrance.

Calling your name,
bluebirds carry your agile mind
over rooftops, their flight toppling
limitations that do not exist.
Your heart travels in winter
always twisted in frozen grins.

Calling your name,
music empties out your puckered mouth
meddling in celestial spheres
where sound escalates and fingers tense,
where even forest animals cling to silence
listening for a hunter's trap.

Calling your name
does nothing for the end of love.
Yet dolphins leap in salty waters
their wet skin shining in the moonlight.
To shore up, store up times past
is the duty of neighbors crossing paths.

Journey

Armadillos in the desert crack and squeak
as they waddle past boll weevil.
It is a silent culture that fits between
scarce sightings, nothing like the screech of train tracks
and a multitude of bodies hovering on a ledge,
huddled together en masse beneath 42nd Street.
In the yellow wasteland, I am eleven years old,
dry sand scorching, shadows cast off spiny cacti.
Atop a lonely boulder, the distance is indefinite
and my long legs dangling feel the heat.
Forever is on the horizon and nothing else.
Old now, the walls of in between seep slowly
into my character so that the desert and city
have crystallized, live in tandem, seal lost pasts.

Holiday

Middling forecast of the future
entwined succinctly with the world,
still, life lifts for the upcoming season.
Less the snow that dusts northern cities,
a festive air permeates local color
and cheery smiles bedeck curious faces.
We share this spell. It is a child's time,
yet who wholly outwits the stage?
It smells of never-perishing evergreens.
Winter is marked by its merry mask.
Deepest in its recesses, despair's shadow
notwithstanding, Christmas is a remedy.
Simple reminder and refresher, more than a day,
the year culminates with baubles and balance.
Sway in its religion, offer up its modesty.

H-O-M-E

Wishes have a way about them
solemn caprice, long-suffering hungers,
aspirations, wants. Lost to children,
wishes then have no hope. There is
no future sentiment, just truth.
A trinket for the wrist, a toy, a pup
contain the dream's answer.
And that mere apparition is sufficient.
But wait, a few more years and yearning
for the outcome, perhaps fulfillment
of visions cut short and new ideas
adapting, become molded into thick rejections.
It is a new era.
Words emerge from a child's mouth.
Miraculous natural sentiments blow into
atmospheric context and mundane
conversations grow significant.
They have music and tonality, breadth,
warmth, life, and a simple merger
of the question and the wish.
"Where do you want to go next?"
Boy aligns with quest, seeking extra.
Girl wishes for the end of provocation.

Mattress

Bassinet cradled in a green grove
carries infant on its soft crepe skin
when leaves flutter and suckling sleeps.

Twin cases side by side where siblings
share nightmares,
and use their beds for circumvention.

Bedded on a wedding eve
cruel and indifferent,
the muslin sheeting chafes.

Mattress, part dream, part comfort,
a box of springs and dimity,
rest for bones, and escape.

Retiring, reclining on a day-bed,
cotton quilt covers knees.
It is perpetual serenity.

Evolution

Kaleidoscopic childhoods
rival Hubble views of space
but milky-colored lusts
amassed in secret mind-cavities
and psychedelic treks
replace a waning youth,
erasing wonderment.
It is how we grow from tadpoles--
making mental picks
like which yellow dog deserves our love.
Ripening through work and middle age
settling, settling
we give up zeal, exhausted
from the upstream swim.
The hoary-headed citizen
if graced by shelf-life
lifts this gloom and points
again to fluid stars, glitter.

ASCENDING

» Creativity

Fame

This is for the dead,
poets of suicidal drift
lured by dark mutterings
at the tip of tongues.

The crowd bellows, bleats
incited by shrill throat-screams
drum-beats, loud guitars,
and they bump their frenzied bodies
against sweet-sweated flesh
until the band collapses, done.
This youth expend themselves
through zealous carnal conduct
but the sober poet
growls
sees the stuff of hazard,
grave-making risk
and through the envy, awe, respect
chronicles the facts
digested with the bile of bearing
historic acts
tinged with pretence
for the sake of seed.

Faded

Sated on greens and plum tomatoes
no meat, no drink, no substance
thin girls sway in men's eyes,
reward for elderly poets.
Today a smoking bard
would never spend all hours
at a winery in philosophical chats.
More likely he's a dad with Volvo, and a
businessman in debt; a drunk's romance
no longer fits the generation.
And self-indulgent intoxications
move backward, dissipating
like 50s rock and roll. The howl
once hell-fired now whimpers,
less thorn than wilted rose.

Georgia

Weeks.
It has been that long
and not a jot of ink
stains a virgin
page.

I touched it
My hand slid on the surface
on its own volition
at home, at rest
again.

The landscape in the Taos hills
dotted
with O'Keefe's green shrubs
coaxing the craft
out.

Hope

Opting out of effort
it seemed like all my talent
was teetering away,
emanating from a voided stomach,
all my blooded veins, drained.

Exiting from the sepulcher
there came a thrift in emotion, composure
and peace was back
where children swing airborne
on a playground begging:
"Watch me, watch me fly!"

Step, step up
lift the pen, the lens, the brush.
Capture the soul of a green fragile weed
pushed up between the cracks
of wintry concrete.

It is similar,
as Spring and creation
spread wings
mend, revive, replicate.

Illustration

See
speak
enter an agreement
with Leonardo's spirit
to smile at brushstrokes
on a painter's board
and the ingenuity of man
to extract indigo
from plant life.

It is a rich hue,
a picture that
feels like velvet
stroked
or a bare shoulder
to the back of a young hand.

It feels like a squeezed fruit dripping juice,
the sweet liquor tasting
cool.
When eyes close they do not
see
how its liquid skirts the mouth
falling
staining a white cotton blouse.

A breeze blows.
Hear the papers drift
through air, hit the floor, slide and settle.
The movement speaks.
See
the art of darkness.

ASCENDING

» Love

Alone?

Resting in an easy, agreeable room,
sounds come from the neighbor's rise
to floor 3
echoing strong ascending footsteps
and a sudden pause.
2 garbled baritones
exchange a gay repertoire.
Then creaking stair boards hum again
and stop.
The silence booms and brings attention
to a lack of company.
No partner, no conversation
no exchange.

At Bamiyan
eating mint and yoghurt pasta
the Afghan, so many years ago,
confided that this loneliness
was ill-taken.
Accepted –
yet there is the passion
of one's own intentions.

Force

Pressure crafts a shining jewel.
It takes years.
Unlike the heart,
it is the best talisman for boys
luring love into a whirlwind courtship,
earthy thrusts and giddy nights
pleasure traps
exotic nuance aimed only at a beloved.
Then, take the bonsai
shrunk to perfect size
for admiration at close range.
If an object of devotion
could be fit into such small bed
great fantasies would rise
higher than fact.
If will alone would rule,
you could be my gentle conqueror
I your lady
steeped in everlasting stain.

Passion

Wine, arms, stars, sacrifice
riding dirt road ditches
bumped up against smooth, hot flesh
we are grounded by touch.

Diminished, skin's sweet fire
erupts in its failing,
clinging to fictions
sweat, toes, dawn, repentance.

Old minds eating brightness
peer back in time
for the capture, squeeze, caress
we once longed to practice, endless.

Retrospective

In summertime when it is slow
I see your shadow.
Promises along Drum River
sizzle off hot earth
scattering, fractioning humid heat
slightly.
That hint of sweat,
that wicked titter,
your gestures
burn like love, seared as scars.

Dreaming

From the twilight of half-sleep
reluctantly I rouse a semi-conscious body
from a warm bed,
splash cool fresh water over a bitter face,
take all the stockpiled rheum from wet eyes
and marvel at the trillionth dream,
still hovering around a sleepy mind,
unique as a snowflake.

I follow you through marshland grass
whacking the dense brush aside
with naked arms
scurrying to catch your confident speed,
fearing to be left in an unknown zone
alone
when there in the distance, the bluest sky
shows itself attainable.
We board a free farm bus spotted with immigrants
and wait forever for our brilliant journey home.

It is a slow awakening
as real attention to a shining sun
breaks into the field of vision.
I am outside once again
alert
ready for the magnificent summoning of God.

Almost

Deep below a bubbling surface rings a half-tone,
notes barely heard and waiting for release
to be pulled headlong into a fury of waters.
I go to you, a disappearing madman
just out of reach, a hair's breadth away.
Sing me that melancholy dialogue
as I must soon devour my desire.
It is almost. Once again it is almost time
to fuse, to ponder dreams
while desperate for sleep.

Cry, cry--
our destiny is blank
and impediments have been placed on our path.
Reach out dry hands
that dissolve like snowflakes' aftermath
and swear this vow so our faces greet at sunrise
while the swell is on the wave.
Grab what's left of promise.
It is almost.

Freedom

In Avon, in Douglasville, the fruit is sweet.
It is where I hear piano keys and dove's
wings flapping through sycamores. You walk
patiently among the Bradford Pears whose scent
leaves an ugly mark hidden in its white beauty.
And I ask for your forgiveness like a naughty child
whose wish it is to be done with fault.
You keep walking, and I catch your curls,
a glint of sun streaming off their darkness.
Turn, I pray, and sigh deeply while the dew freezes.
Distraction pulls all senses toward the past
and it goes unnoticed that you slip off the brier path,
free falling like the weight of eons loosed from your eyes.

Union

Through the teeth
a slow breath whispers,
meets your anticipation
so close it hardly stops
believing in itself.
One eternal kiss
to be our history.
If failing after that
is certain
no worries, no sorrow
as now those carefree few mind-flashes
will linger on the periphery, deathless
as long as spirit tramps
its solitary path, its roaming search
for union.

Glow

Glow-   ing
from the inside.

Smile-less, a face that knows no smile
is the true heart.

I can feel the shiver
of love

in visual silence, as if it were a blinding light

searing heat into my skin, erupting like July explosions

illuminating the unfathomable
sky.

Song

Melancholy mood usurps a tendency to act
as I stare into the starry blue firmament.
No one hears the twinkle of sky-lights.
Can you listen to the soul of a falling leaf
or is it too close to the scratch at your heart?
Higher, we reach until an unbearable ache
pumps up and down like a breath,
and deep scars halt new words from forming.
Words that cleanse, pave a portion of hope
on our treacherous path. Reach. Reach out
a hand and I might play and float beyond
false blues that settle us. Reach my mind in a kind
of lagoon, a tropic that surrounds with green,
lush green curtains of embracing scent.
If I could sing, our voice would rise and rise.

- Title: *Cracked*
- Author: Alice Shapiro
- Price: $14.95
- Publisher: TotalRecall Publications, Inc.
- Format: PaperBack, 6" x 9"
- Number of pages: 112
- 13-digit ISBN: 978-1-59095-835-3
- Publication Date: April 1, 2010
- Distribution arrangements:
  Ingram, Amazon.com, Barnes and Noble, etc.
- Publicity contact information:
  Bruce Moran, 281-992-3131
  Terri Mitchem, 352-596-1192

Alice Shapiro's poems in "Cracked" explore the complex relationships we have as humans to one another, and to the world. With strong images and gripping words, the poems in this book compel us to look at the ordinary and the extraordinary in our own lives. The eloquent use of metaphor in each poem leaves the reader wanting more, turning the page, to find wonderful creativity and surprises in language. The poetry in this collection, does indeed, bring the reader to examine the cracks of our inner and outer worlds. With precision and imagery, the poet finds the waiting spaces inside each of us.

-- Connie Post   Livermore Poet Laureate